FINGERPRINT
our world

Let's Get Started!

Are you ready for a fingerprint adventure? This book is packed with exciting scenes for you to decorate using just your fingerprints and a pen.

Follow the instructions below and learn how to create people, animals, and vehicles.

Grab your ink pad and let's get creative!

You will need:

- A dark-colored pen
- A small cup of water to clean your fingers before changing colors
- A paper towel to dry your hands
- Colored pens for extra details

Add the lines!

Add the colors!

Follow the steps below to learn how to create your own fingerprint friends.
Use lots of different colors and add detail with a dark pen.

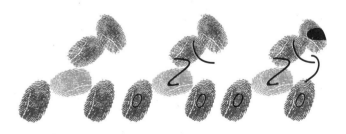

Take a Country Walk

Fill the meadow with sheep and lambs.
Add flowers, butterflies, and bugs.

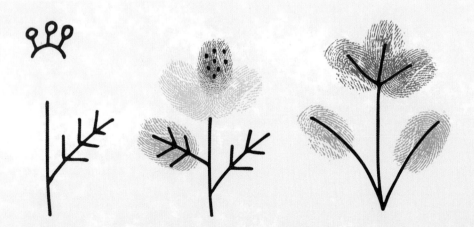

Use lots of different colors for the flowers.

Set Sail for Adventure

Decorate the boats with lots of different colors.
Add some submarines and big ships.

Splash in the Rain

Paint lots of brightly colored umbrellas.
Fill the trees with red and green leaves.

Add raindrops to the sky.

Add puddles to the ground.

Have a Picnic in the Park

What yummy treats are there to eat?
Watch out for pesky ants!

Add lots of fruit!

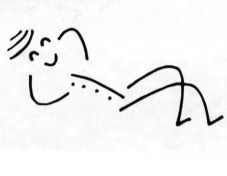

Draw a trail of ants!

Go Diving!

Swim with dolphins and jellyfish, and discover brightly colored tropical fish.

Add lots of coral.

Water in the Red Sea is warm all year round!

Paint bubbles using your little finger.

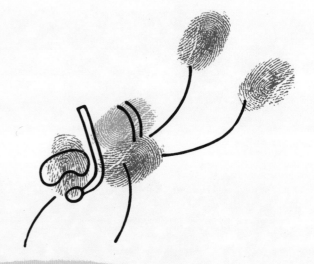

Add shells to the seafloor!

Take a Safari

How many different animals can you spot?
Use a dark pen to add detail.

Watch out for crocodiles!

Add lots of zebras and elephants.

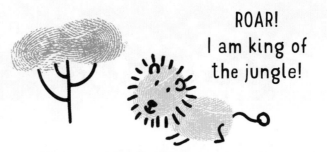

ROAR!
I am king of
the jungle!

I live in a big herd!

Zoom Through a Busy City

Trucks, cars, and motorcycles all share the roads.
What vehicles will you add?

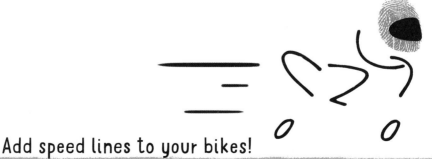

Add speed lines to your bikes!

Hit the Slopes

Zoom down the mountain on skis or a snowboard. Bundle up to keep warm!

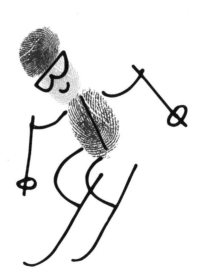

Give everyone gloves, scarves, and hats.

Ski lifts take you high up the mountain.
Add more people to the lift!

Catch a Wave!

Hit the beach and have some fun.
Watch out for sharks!

Surfing makes me happy!

Wahooooooooooooooooooo!

Go Camping!

Time to relax and roast marshmallows. Use red and yellow ink to paint campfires for your campers to sit around.

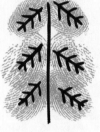

Add some big fish!

Mmmmm, toasty!

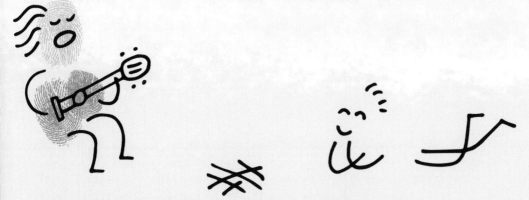

Add details like musical notes and flowers.

Visit the Jungle

Take a boat trip deep into the jungle.
How many animals can you spot?

I love to hang out!

I'm hungry!

Me too!

Explore Underground

These dark caves are home to lots of lovely bats.
Paint bright yellow lights to show the way.

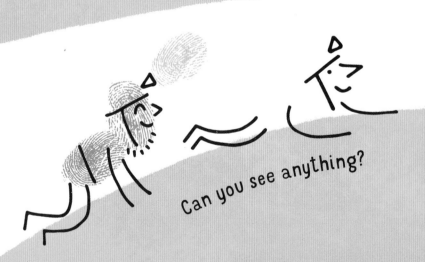

Can you see anything?

Dripping minerals cause the rocks to grow in points. Add some more!

Add bats flying around.

Take a Skydive

See the world from above as you parachute back down to Earth through the clouds. Watch out for birds!

Decorate the parachutes with bright patterns.

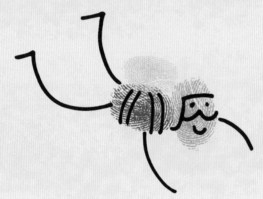

Wheeeeeeeeee!

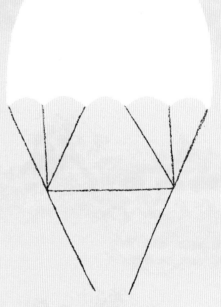

Add birds in every color.

Hit the Beach

Explore the tide pools, and add lots of crabs and fish.
Build some sandcastles on the beach.

Catch!

Draw flags on your castles with a black pen.

Go on an Adventure

Sail through the sky in
a hot-air balloon.
Where will you go?

Decorate your
balloon with
lots of bright
colors.

Add some trees!